Mason Jar Meals

Amazingly Delicious And Easy To Make Recipes For Meals On The Go

Sara Banks

Symbol LLC

Table Of Contents

MASON JAR MEALS

TABLE OF CONTENTS

INTRODUCTION

MASON JAR: A SOLUTION TO MANY OF OUR PROBLEMS

BREAKFAST

MAIN DISHES

SOUPS

DESSERTS

CONCLUSION

FREE PREVIEW MASON JAR SALADS

Introduction

I want to thank you and congratulate you for purchasing the book "Mason Jar Meals-Amazingly Delicious And Easy To Make Recipes For Meals On The Go.

Chances are you have a busy lifestyle that effects what you eat and when you eat. If you are tired of eating processed junk food all the time or skipping meals completely then join the growing crowd who are using mason jars to store great food and eat on the go!

Inside this recipe book you will get loads of great quality recipes ranging from snacks to lunches and dinners. So take control over your eating habits and start enjoying some amazing mason jar meals!

Thanks again!

Sara Banks

Mason Jar: A Solution To Many Of Our Problems

Virtually everyone wants to enjoy a nice meal, as food is what drives us. Actually, failure to have proper meals and a balanced diet contributes to the many complications that we face today. However, our lifestyles simply don't allow us to have the luxury to make food especially due to our busy work schedules such that it becomes almost impossible to even find time to cook or do some other activities. What happens after that is that we end up eating junk and other processed foods, which are often quite expensive. This in turn eats into our savings and even puts us at the risk of various health complications that come with failing to eat a balanced diet or failing to eat at all. For instance, it isn't uncommon for most of us to overcompensate on meals when we skip one or two meals. Since most of us overcompensate at night when just before going to bed, we end up storing too much fat because we actually don't burn much of the food we eat during sleep, which in turn results to many of the complications that we have today. What if I told you that you could stop missing meals and not worry about eating expensive junk, which ends up making you obese, overweight and even puts your life at risk due to intake of processed foods and bad fats? With mason jars, you can prepare your meals when you are free then pack them in the mason jars, and keep them refrigerated until when you need them; that's so easy! You could even store the meals for up to a week, which means that you simply need a few hours in a single day of the week to prepare meals for the entire week then kiss goodbye the habit of missing meals or having to eat junk. I have prepared some delicious and easy to make mason jar meals for breakfast, desserts, soups and main dishes to help you get started to a new lifestyle of having packed snacks, desserts, beverages, lunches, dinners and soups just to mention a few.

Breakfast

Creamy Pumpkin Spice Overnight Oatmeal

Servings: 1

Ingredients

A dash of pumpkin spice (ginger, nutmeg and cinnamon)

½ cup of almond milk

¼ cup of pumpkin puree

¼ cup of steel cut oats

Directions

Combine the ingredients in a bowl and then pour into a mason jar before covering with a lid then let it stay overnight. You can warm in a microwave for about 1 minute to eat or eat while cold.

Crust less Quiche in a Jar

Servings: 8 quiches

Ingredients

½ teaspoon of freshly ground pepper

1 teaspoon of salt

1 cup of half-and-half

12 eggs

Butter (for greasing the jars)

Fillings (choose any of these)

Option 1: Rosemary Tomato-needs some extra preparation time

4 ounces of crumbled feta

1 teaspoon of fresh rosemary that is torn into small pieces

2 cups of onions, halved and thinly sliced

1 tablespoon of butter

8 tomatoes

Or

Broccoli cheddar

¼ teaspoon of nutmeg

6 ounces of sharp cheddar, grated

20 ounces of frozen broccoli florets

Or

Pea and leek filling

¾ cup of shredded parmesan

½ teaspoon of fresh thyme

4 sliced medium leeks (the white and the light green parts only)

1 tablespoon of butter

2 cups of frozen peas, thawed

Directions

Make your quiches according to the instructions below:

Start by pre-heating your oven to 350 degrees F and lightly butter the mouth wide mason jars then transfer them to a rimmed baking sheet. Beat the salt, half and half, the pepper and the eggs in a medium bowl then mix in the prepared fillings, the spices or herbs as listed in your preferred quick flavor.

Divide the ingredients using a ladle among the 8 mason jars. Bake for up to 40 minutes or until set and golden at the top then allow to cool completely before covering with the lids and refrigerating.

Preparing the fillings:

The rosemary tomato

If you use this filling, the roasting will take another 45 minutes of preparation time. Preheat the oven to 450 degrees°F then line 2 baking sheets with some parchment paper and then slice the tomatoes and spread them over the baking sheets. Roast these for about 45 minutes or until most of the liquid is gone and the tomatoes start to caramelize. Once the tomatoes are properly cooked, chop them roughly. In the mean time, heat a pan over medium-high heat then melt 1 tablespoon of butter and sauté the onions for about 10 minutes or until they are soft and golden. Remove these from heat and set them aside.

The broccoli cheddar

Boil salted water in a large pot then add in the broccoli florets and cook them for about 1 minute, drain them well and remove any extra water with paper towels and chop them roughly.

Pea & Leek

Heat a pan over medium-high heat and then melt 1 tablespoon of butter and sauté the leeks for about 10 minutes or until soft and set them aside.

Amaretto Cocoa Mix

Servings: 8 jars

What you need

8 mason jars (1 pint)

½ teaspoon of salt

2 ¾ cups of non-dairy powdered creamer

3 ½ cups of Nestlé's quick

2 jars (8 ounces) of amaretto flavored powdered creamer (non-dairy)

4 cups of confectioners' sugar

10 ½ cups of non-fat dry milk

Directions

Mix all the ingredients and divide evenly among the jars. To serve mix 3 tablespoons of the cocoa mix in a cup of water or milk.

Spiced Mocha Mix

Servings: 1

Ingredients

¼ Teaspoon of nutmeg

¼ cup of sugar

1/3 cup of instant coffee

½ cup of cocoa mix

½ cup of powdered coffee cream

¼ teaspoon cinnamon

Directions

Place all the ingredients in a bowl and combine them well then transfer the mixture into a mason jar. When serving, add 2 tablespoons of the mixture to 1 cup of water.

Brownie Cakes in Jar

Servings: 2

Ingredients

¼ cup of walnuts (finely chopped)

½ teaspoon of vanilla extract

1 beaten egg

¼ cup of buttermilk

3 tablespoons of unsweetened cocoa powder

¼ cup of water

1/3 cup of butter/margarine

¼ teaspoon of ground cinnamon

½ teaspoon of baking soda

1 cup of sugar

1 cup of all-purpose flour

2 masons jars wide mouth

Directions

First, pre-heat the oven to 325 degrees F.

Sterilize the mason jars immersing them in boiling water then stir together the cinnamon, flour, baking soda and sugar and then set aside.

Mix margarine or butter, cocoa powder and water in a medium saucepan then heat and stir the mixture on medium heat until all the butter or margarine has melted and everything is properly mixed and then remove from the heat and stir in the flour mixture.

Add the vanilla, egg and the buttermilk then beat by hand until everything is smooth then add in the nuts and pour the mixture into the mason jars. Place the jars on a cookie sheet and then bake at 325 degrees F for about 40 minutes or until a toothpick comes out clean when inserted into the cake.

Remove the cakes from the oven one after the other and place a lid then a ring onto the mason jars and screw down tightly. Put the jars on the counter to cool.

Mason Jar Breakfast Parfait

Servings: 1

Ingredients

2 tablespoons of flax seed meal (ground)

½ cup vanilla Greek yoghurt

½ cup of granola

¼ cup of raspberries

¼ cup of blueberries

Directions

Spoon about ¼ cup of the Greek yogurt into a Mason jar then pour in about ¼ cup of granola over the yogurt and then add in one tablespoon of the ground flaxseed meal. Layer the mixture with raspberries and blueberries then spoon the remaining ¼ cup of Greek yogurt over the fruit, top with the remaining granola then add another tablespoon of the flax seed meal and then finally top with the raspberries and blueberries.

Applesauce Cake in a Jar

Servings: 3

Ingredients

2 2/3 cups of sugar

2/3 cups of chopped nuts

2/3 cup of shortening

½ teaspoon of baking powder

2 teaspoons of ground cloves

1 teaspoon of cinnamon

1 ½ teaspoon of salt

2 teaspoons of baking soda

3 1/3 cups of sifted, all-purpose flour

2/3 cups of water

2 cups of applesauce

4 eggs

Directions

Start with pre-heating the oven to 325 ºF and then sterilize your mason jars in boiling water for at least 15 minutes; keep everything in the boiling water until you want to use them. When you remove the jars from the boiling water, place them on a clean dishtowel to allow it to dry up while facing up and not upside down.

When the jars have cooled, grease their inside walls with the shortening and then set them aside.

Sift the baking powder, the salt, baking soda, cinnamon, cloves and flour together then set aside.

Cream together the sugar and the shortening and then beat in the eggs one at a time until the mixture is fluffy and light enough.

Add in the water and the applesauce then blend the dry ingredients with the applesauce mixture then fold in the chopped nuts, set aside and half fill the well greased jars with the mixture then bake them for about 35-40 minutes at 325 degrees F or until a toothpick comes out clean.

Toasted Oat And Coconut Muesli

Servings: 5

Ingredients

½ teaspoon of freshly grated nutmeg

½ teaspoon of ground cinnamon

¼ cup of chia seeds

1 cup of candied ginger, coarsely chopped

1 cup of dried cranberries

1 cup of coarsely chopped dry roasted almonds

1 cup of unsweetened coconut flakes

1 teaspoon of salt

4 cups of old fashioned oats

Serving:

Pure maple syrup

Cold almond milk

Frozen blueberries

Directions

Put two racks at the center and upper third of oven then preheat oven to 350 degrees F.

Place the oats on unlined and ungreased baking sheet then place the coconuts in another baking sheet that is ungreased and unlined. Toast the oats and the coconut for about 5-7 minutes or until the coconut turns golden brown and is fragrant.

Remove both the coconut and oats from oven and allow them to cool off.

Toss together the oats, spices, chia seeds, cranberries, coconut and the salt in a large bowl then transfer them to air tight jars to store.

Prepare muesli the night before, or at least a few hours before you'd like to serve it. To serve, scoop desired amount of muesli into a bowl. When serving, top it with a handful of frozen blueberries and pour almond milk over the muesli-enough to cover the blueberries then cover and place in the fridge overnight, or for at least 2 hours. When ready to serve drizzle with some pure maple syrup.

Main Dishes

Deconstructed Sushi in a Jar

Servings: 1 wide mouth Mason jar

What you need

1 wide mouth Mason jar

Limejuice

½ avocado (diced)

¼ cup of cucumber matchsticks

¼ cup of shredded carrot

1 sheet of nori (cut into 1 inch by ¼ inch pieces)

2 teaspoons of soy sauce

1 teaspoon of sugar

1 tablespoon of rice vinegar

¾ cup of cooked short grain (brown rice)

Wasabi paste (to taste)

Pickled ginger (to taste)

Directions

In a small saucepan, heat the sugar and vinegar over medium heat until all the sugar dissolves. Pour the sugar and vinegar mixture and soy sauce over the rice while the brown rice is still warm then toss well to combine and let them cool to room temperature.

*Omit sugar and heat if you use seasoned rice vinegar.

Cut the nori into small pieces using a knife. Use ¼ cups of carrot for lunch or 2 medium size carrots to make six lunches. After preparing the vegetables, place the avocado in a small bowl then toss with lime juice until coated well to prevent browning.

Once your ingredients are ready, add a layer at a time then level and pat down each layer using a spoon. Arrange the ingredients in the following order:

First layer (bottom)-1/2 sheet nori

Second layer- ½ cup of rice

Third layer- ¼ cup of carrot

Fourth layer- ¼ cup of rice

Fifth layer- pickled ginger

Sixth layer- ½ avocado

Seventh layer - ½ cup of rice

Eighth layer - ¼ cup cucumber

Ninth layer - ½ sheet nori

Finish with ginger and wasabi tasting.

Jalapeno, Creamed Corn And Cheddar Cornbread

Servings: 3

Ingredients

1 cup of shredded sharp cheddar cheese

2 medium jalapenos (diced finely)

1/3 cup of grated onion

1 cup of creamed corn

2 eggs

1 cup of buttermilk

½ teaspoon baking soda

2 teaspoons of baking powder

1 teaspoon of salt

2 cups of yellow cornmeal

Directions

Whisk the cornmeal, the salt, the baking powder, and the baking soda in a medium bowl. In another larger bowl, whisk the butter milk, the eggs, the onion, the creamed corn and jalapeno. When well combined, add dry ingredients to wet mixture and stir vigorously. Lastly, fold in the cheese.

Fill a wide mouth mason jar with a cup of leftover chili then scoop 1/3 of cup plus one heaping tablespoon of cornbread batter over the chili. Bake for around 25 minutes or until a toothpick inserted at the center comes out clean. It is best to let the jars to cool completely before covering them with the lids.

Thai Peanut Tofu Spread

Yield: 5 cups

Ingredients

1/3 cup of chopped peanuts or cashews

1 bunch of scallions (thinly sliced)

½ cup of chopped cilantro

¾ cup of finely diced bell pepper

1 cup of shredded carrot

3 tablespoons of sugar

2 tablespoons of rice vinegar

1/3 cup of tamari

1 teaspoon chili paste

½ cup of coconut milk

½ cup of peanut butter

2 peeled cloves of garlic

1 ½ inch piece of ginger (quartered and peeled)

20 ounces of extra firm tofu (high protein)

Directions

Squeeze the extra liquid out of the tofu. Use two cutting boards to slice the tofu longitudinally into two thin pieces and wrap them in a clean kitchen towel that will help in absorbing the excess liquid. You need to do this so as to make sure the tofu will absorb the recipe liquid instead. Pulse the garlic and the ginger in a food processor until minced finely. Open the processer from time to time and scrap down the sides and process again until you are satisfied it is all well processed. Add the chili paste, the peanut butter, the coconut milk, sugar, rice vinegar and tamari. Pulse in the food processor until well blended, this will take around one minute.

Split the tofu into several small pieces then add them to the peanut mixture. Process in the food processor until the mixture is well blended and the tofu should be chopped into smaller pieces by this time. Place the remaining mixture in a medium bowl and fold them in the rest of the ingredients.

You can pack a mason jar with around ½ a cup of the tofu spread in ½ jar pint Mason jar together with a mason jar of cucumbers and carrots then add another half-pint with whole wheat flat bread.

Preserved lemon pasta

Servings: 8

Ingredients

4 ounces of pecorino (shredded)

¾ cup of flat leave parsley (chopped)

1 (15-ounce) can of chickpeas

½ cup of halved Moroccan olives (pitted)

1 cup of reserved pasta cooking water (divided)

3 yolks of egg

¼ teaspoon of red pepper flakes

1/8 teaspoon of turmeric

1 cup of dry white wine

4 cloves of garlic (minced)

1 red onion, medium (halved and sliced thinly)

3 tablespoons of olive oil

1 (15 ounce) whole grain pasta package

½ cup preserved lemon pulp and peel, diced

Directions

Cook pasta as per the package cooking instructions then when cooked, drain and reserve a cup of the starchy cooking water of the pasta. In the meantime, heat a sauté pan over medium heat and then add the olive oil. When the oil has heated, put the onions and sauté until they turn translucent for about 8 minutes. Add garlic and then sauté for an extra one minute. Add the turmeric, the wine, and the pepper flakes and bring to a simmer. Reduce the heat and cook until the liquid is half the initial amount and it looks slightly thick.

Whisk the egg yolks in a small bowl and slowly pour in ½ cup of the reserved pasta cooking water as you continue whisking. Make sure there are no lumps then add the eggs mixture into the sauce and continue cooking on low heat until slightly thick for about 3 minutes. Remove from the heat and toss the sauce with noodles. For the sauce to coat easily to the pasta, use as much pasta cooking water as possible. Add the preserved lemon, the olives, the parsley, and the pecorino then toss until well blended. Put this into your jars and refrigerate.

Polenta with Cream Cheese and Chives

Servings: 6 pint-sized mason jars

Ingredients

2 tablespoons of chives (chopped)

6 tablespoons of cream cheese

1 cup of yellow cornmeal

1 teaspoon of salt

4 cups of water

Directions

Bring water and salt to boil in a medium sauce pan, and then add the cornmeal slowly as you continue whisking. Lower the heat to low and then simmer for about 10 minutes and keep stirring constantly until it is thick. Remove from the heat and stir it in cream cheese and the chives until it is fully combined. Divide the mixture between six mason jars of pint size then let it cool and refrigerate to set.

Irish Shepherd's Pie

Servings: six wide mouth mason jars

Ingredients

For malcannon topping

1/8 teaspoon of freshly ground nutmeg

¾ teaspoon of salt

1 ½ tablespoons of butter

¾ cup of milk

1 leek (sliced) light green and white parts only

3 cups of packed chopped kale (de-stemmed)

3 medium Yukon gold potatoes (1 pound)

For the filling

¼ cup of chopped parsley (flat- leaf)

1 cup of frozen peas (thawed)

2 teaspoons of vegetarian Worcestershire

½ cup of vegetable broth

½ cup of Guinness

2 tablespoons of flour

½ teaspoon of freshly ground pepper

½ teaspoon of salt

1 bay leaf

1 cup of chopped cabbage

2 medium carrots (finely chopped)

3 finely chopped leaves of celery

2 cloves of garlic, minced

1 medium onion (chopped)

1 ½ tablespoons of olive oil (divided)

14 ounces of crumbled vegetarian sausage

Directions

Pre-heat an oven to heat of 400°F.

Meanwhile prepare the colcannon:

Start by peeling the potatoes then chop them into large cubes. Put them in a medium sized pot and cover the pot with water. Over high heat, bring to a simmer then reduce heat to low. Simmer for about 15 minutes until the potatoes break apart when poked with a spoon. Drain the potatoes then return them to pot and mash them before covering.

As the potatoes are cooking, bring the leek, the kale, the milk, the salt, the butter and the nutmeg to a simmer in a pot. Let it remain covered and stir from time to time until soft for about 12 minutes. Add kale mixture to mashed potatoes and the sir to incorporate. Let it remain covered as you prepare the filling.

Prepare Filling:

Heat 1 tablespoon of the olive oil in a pan on medium-high heat. Once the oil is hot, add the sausage and cook until browned. Put the sausage aside in a plate. Place half tablespoon of olive oil in the same pan used for sausage and add garlic, onion, carrot, celery, bay leaf, cabbage, salt and pepper. Sauté for 12 minutes until it is soft then add flour and stir until the veggies are uniformly coated. Add the Guinness, Worcestershire and the broth then cook until bubbly and thick. Put the sausage, the parsley and the peas then continue cooking until well combined and warmed throughout. Remove the bay leaf.

Filling of the jars

Split the filling uniformly between the six wide mouth jars and then divide the colcannon topping uniformly between the jars.

Bake filled jars:

Put jars on a rimmed baking sheet and bake at 400°F for around 20 minutes and then remove the sheet with jars from oven then switch set the oven to broil.

Add the cheese as topping (optional though). Sprinkle a tablespoon at the top of each jar and return the baking sheet and the jars to the oven under broiler. Monitor closely as it broils. Let the cheese turn golden for about 3 minutes. Let it cool totally before putting lids on jars and then store in the fridge.

Mason Jar Barbecue Sundae

Yield: 12 small sized- *mason jars*

Ingredients

1 jar of bread and butter pickles

1 recipe of the crock pot barbecue (explained below)

1 recipe of easy slaw (explained below)

2 cans of baked beans

Directions

Put the beans, the slaw and the barbecue into the jars in that order then top it up with the pickle garnish. The barbecue is ready for serving.

Easy cole slaw

Servings: 4

Ingredients

¼ teaspoon of celery

¼ teaspoon of pepper

½ teaspoon of salt

1 tablespoon of honey

2 tablespoons of mayonnaise

¼ cup of canola oil

¼ cup of apple cider vinegar

1 bag of shredded coleslaw mix

Directions

Whisk all the sauce ingredients. Pour the sauce over the shredded coleslaw mix.

Crockpot barbecue

Servings: 4

Ingredients

½ Teaspoon of paprika

½ teaspoon of chili powder

½ teaspoon of dry mustard

2 tablespoons Worcestershire sauce

¼ cup of lemon juice

¼ cup of butter

¼ cup of brown sugar

½ cup of vinegar

1 chopped sweet onion

12 ounce bottle of chili sauce

A large can of tomato sauce

1 teaspoon of salt

4 pound of roast or 4 pound piece of pork

Include buns in case you are not serving in a jar

Directions

Put the roast in a crock-pot then sprinkle with salt and add some water to cover through. Cook this for 6 hours. In the last hour of cooking, stir together the tomato sauce, chili sauce, vinegar, sweet onion, brown sugar, butter, lemon juice, mustard, Worcestershire sauce, chili powder and paprika in a large pan. Bring to a boil, reduce heat and simmer for about one hour as you keep stirring constantly. Shred the meat and mix with the sauce.

Baked corn dogs in a mason jar

Servings: 12 corn dogs

Ingredients

¾ cup of sugar

½ cup of sour cream

1 ½ cups of milk

¼ cup of oil

6 eggs

3 cups of yellow self-rising corn meal mix

6 hot dogs cut in half (uncured)

Directions

Pre-heat your oven to 375 degrees F, and then mix all the ingredients using a hand mixer except the hot dogs. When the mixture is smooth, pour in 12 greased medium sized mason jars filing about 4 ounces scant. Put the hot dogs standing right at center of batter. Bake this for 20 minutes until the corn bread is golden brown and cooked throughout. Allow to cool then turn stuff a knife around each of the corn dog to loosen from the side of jars. Allow to cool completely, then lid, and put in the fridge until you are ready to serve. When serving, take out of the fridge and remove the lid then microwave for about 45 seconds. You can serve with a side of mustard or ketchup.

Asian noodle salad in a jar

Servings: 4 jars

Ingredients

For peanut dressing

1 tablespoon of black sesame seeds

¼ cup of extra virgin olive oil

4 teaspoons of sauce

4 teaspoons of rice vinegar

4 teaspoons of sambal oelek

2 tablespoons peanut butter

For salad

½ cup of crunchy rice noodles

4 green onions (thinly sliced)

2 large carrots (peeled and shredded)

1 cup (cooked) shelled edamane beans

1 red bell pepper (thinly sliced)

4 ounces of soba noodles

Directions

Cook the noodles according to package directions in large pot of boiling water then rinse and drain under cold water.

In the meantime, prepare a Spicy Peanut Dressing by whisking the rice vinegar, peanut butter, samba oelek and soy sauce. Drizzle in oil while you continue whisking until all the oil is well combined then add in the sesame seeds and stir.

Divide the Peanut Dressing among the four mason jars equally and then divide the soba noodles on top of the dressing. Put the rest of the ingredients in layers ensuring to have the rice noodles at the top. Cover with lids and place in the fridge up to 5 days. When serving put in plate or bowl and stir before serving.

SOUPS

Hearty Soup Mix in a Jar

Servings: 5

Ingredients

Multi-color spiral pasta

¼ cup of rice

¼ cup of lentils

¼ cup of barley

½ cup of small shell pasta, split peas or elbow macaroni

¼ cup of onion flakes

1/3 cup of beef or chicken bouillon cubes

Olive oil

Directions

Using a one quart mason jar, layer the ingredients in the following order, start with the cup of beef or chicken at the bottom of the jar , then followed by the onion flakes, split peas, small shell pasta or macaroni, the barley, lentils, the cup of rice, and top with the multi-color spiral pasta.

Brown a pound of beef in olive oil then remove the multi-color pasta from the jar and set it aside.

Add the other ingredients to a soup kettle that has about 12 cups of water. Allow it to come to a boil and then simmer for about 45 minutes. Add the pasta and then let it simmer for 15 more minutes.

Finally, add the browned beef and serve.

Soup in a jar

Servings: 1

Ingredients

1 cup of uncooked twisted macaroni

½ cup of uncooked alphabet pasta

2 tablespoons of dried parsley

2 tablespoons of dried minced onion

½ cup of dry lentils

½ cup of uncooked rice

2 teaspoons of salt

½ teaspoon of lemon pepper

2 tablespoons of beef bouillon granules

½ cup of dried split peas

½ cup of barley

Directions

In a wide mouth Mason jar, put the ingredients in layers starting with the barley, followed by the peas, the rice, and the lentils. Layer the edges with the onion, the parsley, the salt, the lemon pepper, the bouillon and then the alphabet pasta. Lastly, fill the remaining space of the jar with the macaroni.

Cheese Soup Jar Mix

Servings: 4

Ingredients

2 cups of instant potato flakes

½ teaspoon of pepper

1 teaspoon dried minced onion

1 tablespoon of chicken bouillon granules

1 tablespoon of dried parsley flakes

½ cup of powdered cheese sauce mix

½ cup of imitation bacon bits

2 cups of instant coffee creamer

Directions

Place the soup mix in a bowl and add to it 5 cups of boiling water. Let it sit for some minutes before you garnish it if you wish. Pack it in a jar if you wish to consume it later.

Confetti Soup Jar Mix

Servings: 5

Ingredients

1 cup-tri color spiral pasta

1/3 cup of long grain white rice

1 dried bay leaf

1 teaspoon dried basil

½ teaspoon garlic salt

1 teaspoon dried thyme

½ cup of dried lentils

¼ cup of barley

½ cup of dried split peas

¼ cup of dried minced onions

1/3 cup of beef bouillon granules

Directions

Boil all the ingredients in 5 cups of water (adjust water according to your needs). Ensure pasta and rice is well cooked before transferring it into 5 mason jars.

Desserts

Mason Jar No-Bake Cheesecake

Servings: 5

Ingredients

1 tablespoon of lemon juice

½ cup of chocolate chips

¾ pounds of strawberries

2 tablespoons of white sugar

½ cup of sweetened condensed milk

1 brick (8-ounce) cream cheese

1/8 of teaspoon cinnamon

3 tablespoons of butter

1 ¼ cups of Graham Crumbs

1 teaspoon vanilla extract

Directions

For graham crust

Put the crumbs in a medium sized bowl then stir in some little bit of sugar. Stir in melted butter until they are all well combined then set these aside.

For cheesecake filling

Set an electric mixer at medium-high speed and beat cream cheese in a bowl until it is smooth. Beat in condensed milk bit by bit as you scrap the walls of the bowl when necessary.

Mix in the vanilla and the lemon juice.

Put half of the crumb mixture into the mason jars (use 5 1 cup jars) then place some chocolate chips on the crumb.

Pour in some of the cheesecake mixture and then put strawberries on top. Sprinkle the remaining mixture and end with strawberries.

Let it chill in the refrigerator for not less than 2 hours. Drizzle with some chocolate syrup on the top when you serve.

Nutella Mousse Peanut Butter Cups

Servings: 8

Ingredients

Cool whip

1 cup of butter

3 tablespoons of peanut butter

2 cups of crushed chocolate wafers

1 packet (1.34 ounce) of instant chocolate pudding

¼ cup of sugar

1 ¼ cup of fast free milk (avoid whole milk)

¼ cup of nutella

Directions

In preparing the peanut butter crust:

In a food processor, crush one packet of chocolate wafers to pulverize them. Combine 2 cups of the crushed wafers with the melted butter (use a microwave to nuke), 2 heaping tablespoonfuls of peanut butter and the sugar. Layer at the bottom of mason jars and bake at 375 degrees F for about 10 minutes.

Preparing the Nutella mousse:

Whisk dry the instant chocolate pudding mix with the milk vigorously for about 2 minutes then add in the ¼ cup of Nutella and then whisk for 2 more minutes before adding in ½ of the cool whip (4 ounce) and whisk further for 3 more minutes.

Carefully fold in the rest of the cool whip using a spatula and pour into the jars on top of the peanut butter crust. Let it sit for 4 hours. Add the dressing and serve with dollop of cool whip topped with peanut butter chips and crushed chocolate wafer crumbs.

Chocolate Eclair Cake in a Jar

Servings: 3

Ingredients

1 cup of cool whip (thawed)

3 cups of milk

2 boxes of vanilla instant pudding (small)

Graham crackers

For the frosting

1 teaspoon of vanilla

2 tablespoons of softened butter

1 cup of sugar

1/3 cup of unsweetened cocoa

½ cup of milk

Directions

Combine the pudding together with 3 cups of milk in a large bowl and stir using a whisk until it is thick then refrigerate for about 5 minutes for good consistency of the pudding and then fold in the cool whip.

Put 5 graham crackers in a large bag and slowly crush using the back of a spoon. Add enough graham crackers crumbs to the bottom of a mason jar to make a visible layer.

To the graham cracker layer, top with pudding mixture then put another layer of graham cracker crumbs followed by another layer of pudding mixture again. Do this repeatedly until the jar is full but make sure that the pudding layer is the last on top. Put the jars in the fridge as you are preparing the frosting.

Boil the milk in a heavy saucepan while stirring frequently with a whisk then whisk in the sugar and the cocoa and then boil for 2 minutes as you whisk constantly. Set the heat to low and whisk in the vanilla and butter. To create the chocolate tops, pour this milk mixture into the jars and refrigerate for not less than an hour or until set.

Triple Berry and Nut Salad in a Jar

Servings: 4

What you need

1 cup of roasted almonds (roughly chopped)

2 cups of blue berries

2 cups of black berries

2 hulled cups of strawberries (quartered)

4 mason jars (12 ounce)

Sweet Citrus Dressing

2 tablespoons olive oil

¼ cup of orange juice

1 tablespoon of honey

1 whole lemon (juice and zest)

Directions

Make the dressing by mixing orange juice, olive oil, zest, lemon juice and honey in a small bowl and whisk until it is combine well then set aside. In each Mason jar, arrange the ingredients in the order below:

1st layer (Bottom): Place 3 tablespoons of citrus dressing

2nd layer: Place ½ cup of the blackberries

3rd layer: Place ½ cup of strawberries

4th layer: Place ½ cup of blueberries

5th layer (top): Place ¼ cup of almonds.

Refrigerate until you are prepared to eat. Serve by dumping the contents into a bowl then toss.

Chocolate Jar Cakes

Servings: 8

What you need

¾ cups of unsweetened cocoa powder

3 cups of flour

2 cups of unsweetened applesauce

1 tablespoon of vanilla

4 eggs

3 cups of sugar

1 stick plus 3 tablespoons of butter (unsalted)

½ teaspoon of baking powder

8 pint-sized wide mouth Mason jars

1/8 teaspoon of salt

1 teaspoon of baking soda

Directions

Wash the mason jars well in hot soapy water, rinse them properly, dry them and let them cool to room temperature.

Pre-heat the oven to 325 degrees F.

Grease the insides of the mason jars then beat together half of the sugar and the butter until it is fluffy.

Add the rest of the sugar, applesauce, eggs and vanilla. Sift dry all ingredients and then add in the applesauce mixture a little at a time ensuring to mix well with each addition. Pour about 1 cup of batter into every jar then remove then wipe off any that might be on the rims.

Put the mason jars in a oven preheated at 325 degrees F and bake for at least 40 minutes. As the cakes bake, boil water in a saucepan then add in the jar lids, boil for a minute and then remove the pan from heat; ensure to keep the lids in the hot water until ready to use. When the cakes are done baking, take the jars out of the oven. Make sure the jar rims are clean for a proper seal. The cakes will slide out of the mason jars when ready to serve.

S'mores in a jar

Servings: 2

What you need

1 ¼ cups of chocolate chips

1/3 cup of brown sugar (packed)

A large pack of seasonal marshmallow candies

1 ½ cups of crushed graham crackers

1 Mason jar quart sized with a lid and ring

Directions

Put the graham crackers in a zipper freezer food bag then use meat tenderizer or rolling pin to crush the crackers into small crumbs until you make about 1 ½ cups of crushed crumbs. A sleeve of graham crackers that is about 10 whole crackers is equal to 1 ½ cups in crushed form.

Put the crushed graham crackers into a mason jar and use the meat tenderizer to fill the crumbs tightly into the bottom of the jar then put peeps candies along the walls of the glass sides of the Mason jar and then press a little to create a hollow at the center of the jar. You will use approximately 2/3 of the package.

Now add brown sugar to the space in the center of the peeps and try to press lightly to ensure that it is properly packed.

Add the chocolate chips gently at the top then seal the jar using a sealer ring and lid.

Chocolate Chip Cookie Mix in a Jar

Servings: 2 dozen cookies

Ingredients

½ cup of granulated sugar

1 large egg

¾ cup of packed brown sugar

1 ¾ cups of semisweet chocolate morsels

1 teaspoon vanilla extract

1 ¾ cups of all-purpose flour

½ teaspoon of salt

¾ teaspoon of baking soda

¾ sticks of softened butter or margarine

Cookie mix

½ cup of chopped nuts (optional)

Directions

Combine the salt and the baking soda in a small bowl, and then put the flour mixture in a jar. Put the rest of the ingredients in the following order: the baking soda, the salt, the chocolate morsels, the brown sugar, the granulated sugar and then the all-purpose flour. Pre-heat the oven to 375°F.

Meanwhile, in a large bowl, beat the vanilla extract, egg and butter until well combined.

Put in the cookie mix and ½ cup of chopped nuts. Bake for 11 minutes or until they start turning golden brown then cool on the baking sheets for about 2 minutes. You can then transfer you cookies to the jars, pack them tightly seal and refrigerate for later.

Conclusion

Thank you again for purchasing this recipe book! I hope that you now have some really great ideas and recipes to get you started with mason jar meals. It's important that you focus on your health and nutrition throughout your busy day. It isn't healthy to keep skipping meals and eating so much processed junk food all the time even if you have the excuse of being busy. Spending the time to prepare some great mason jar meals is very rewarding and also fun.

Your next step is to start exploring with the mason jar meals provided and see which one becomes your favorite. I would also recommend that you check out my other book titled **"Mason Jar Salads: Amazingly Healthy and Delicious Recipes For Salads on The Go."** It will be the perfect complement to this book to add some healthy salad options to your busy life on the go.

I have included a free preview on the next page for your viewing pleasure.

Thanks

Sara Banks

Free Preview Mason Jar Salads

Taco Salad Jar

Servings: two mason jars

Ingredients

For salad

Sour cream and cheese

Shredded lettuce or any other green leaf

A small handful cilantro

2 tablespoons of fresh salsa

1 small avocado, diced

½ cup of cooked quinoa

¼ cup of sliced green onions

¼ cup of diced red bell pepper

½ cup of black beans (drained and rinsed)

For cumin-lime vinaigrette

½ teaspoon of ground cumin

2 tablespoons of extra virgin olive oil

1 teaspoon honey

A pinch of salt

3 tablespoons of fresh squeezed lime juice

Directions

Whisk all the vinaigrette ingredients and then pour into the quart-sized jars then layer ingredients for the salad in a jar in the following order: the black beans, the diced pepper, the green onions, the quinoa, the avocado, the fresh salsa, the cilantro, the lettuce and lastly the cream at the top. Close with the lid and put in the fridge until when ready to eat. Consume within 3 days.

When serving, turn the jar over the vinaigrette to coat with the salad ingredients.

Chopped Taco Mason Jar Salad

Servings: 5

Ingredients

5 cups of chopped romaine lettuce

1 (1-ounce) jar jalapenos (drained, pickled and chopped)

5 mini cucumbers (sliced)

1 quart cherry tomatoes (halved)

5 tablespoons plain Greek yoghurt

1 ¼ cup of salsa

1 packet of taco seasoning

1 can of black beans drained

1 pound of ground turkey

5 wide mouth quart size mason jars

Directions

Cook ground turkey over medium heat on a pan, until it is no longer pink then add black beans, the seasoning and the amount of water stated in the seasoning instructions. Allow the taco mixture to cool. Split the ingredients among the mason jars starting with the salsa and then add the Greek yoghurt, the tomatoes, the cucumbers, the onions, the jalapenos, the avocados, the taco meat and then the lettuce. Place a lid on and close tightly; do not vacuum seal or anything like that. Shake well when ready to eat then pour into a bowl to serve. It can be served with tortilla chips.

The salads can be made 5 days ahead of time.............

© Copyright 2014 by Symbol LLC - All rights reserved.

This document is geared towards providing exact and reliable information in regards to the topic and issue covered. The publication is sold with the idea that the publisher is not required to render officially permitted, accounting, or otherwise, qualified services. If advice is necessary, legal or professional, a practiced individual in the profession should be ordered.

- From a Declaration of Principles which was accepted and approved equally by a Committee of the American Bar Association and a Committee of Publishers and Associations.

In no way is it legal to reproduce, duplicate, or transmit any part of this document in either electronic means or in printed format. Recording of this publication is strictly prohibited and any storage of this document is not allowed unless with written permission from the publisher. All rights reserved.

The information provided herein is stated to be truthful and consistent, in that any liability, in terms of inattention or otherwise, by any usage or abuse of any policies, processes, or directions contained within is the solitary and utter responsibility of the recipient reader. Under no circumstances will any legal responsibility or blame be held against the publisher for any reparation, damages, or monetary loss due to the information herein, either directly or indirectly.

Respective authors own all copyrights not held by the publisher.

The information herein is offered for informational purposes solely, and is universal as so. The presentation of the information is without contract or any type of guarantee assurance.

The trademarks that are used are without any consent, and the publication of the trademark is without permission or backing by the trademark owner. All trademarks and brands within this book are for clarifying purposes only and are the owned by the owners themselves, not affiliated with this document.

Printed in Great Britain
by Amazon